DETECTIVE ACADEMY™

Basic Training Manual

by Luke Miller and Paul Mauro
with H. Keith Melton
consultant

Scholastic Inc.
New York • Toronto • London • Auckland • Sydney
Mexico City • New Delhi • Hong Kong • Buenos Aires

Detective Rookies, sign in here!

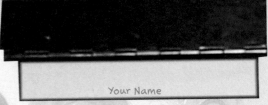

Your Name

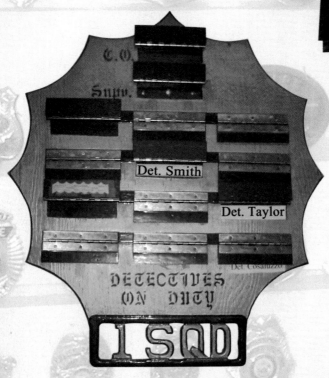

Det. Smith

Det. Taylor

Det. Cosaluzzo

DETECTIVES ON DUTY

1 SQD

Sign-in Board

How do some detectives sign in when they show up for work? Using this sign-in board, they just flip up a section to show their name—and let their fellow detectives know they're on duty! (1 SQD stands for First Detective Squad. You'll learn more about squads in this book!)

No part of this publication may be reproduced in whole or in part, or stored in a retrieval system, or transmitted in any form or by any means, electronic, mechanical, photocopying, recording, or otherwise, without the written permission of the publisher. For information regarding permission, please write to Scholastic Inc., Attention: Permissions Department, 557 Broadway, New York, NY 10012.

ISBN: 0-439-57174-X

Design: Mark Neston

Illustrations: Daniel Aycock, Yancey Labat, Antoine Clarke

Photos: Daniel Aycock, Mark Neston, Catherine Ritz, Lightning Powder Company (pg. 23)

Copyright © 2003 by Scholastic Inc.

All rights reserved. Published by Scholastic Inc.

A special thanks to Detective Mike Singer of the 6th Precinct of the New York Police Department for allowing the editors of this book to hang out at the precinct, ask a lot of questions, and see detectives at work.

SCHOLASTIC, DETECTIVE ACADEMY, and associated logos are trademarks and/or registered trademarks of Scholastic Inc.

12 11 10 9 8 7 6 5 4 3 2 1   3 4 5 6 7 8/0

Printed in the U.S.A.

First Scholastic printing, September 2003

The publisher has made every effort to ensure that the activities in this book are safe when done as instructed. Children are encouraged to do their detective activities with willing friends and family members and to respect others' right to privacy. Adults should provide guidance and supervision whenever the activity requires.

Shields Across America

The background of this page shows photos of police and detective badges from across the country.

Case Log

DA When you see this symbol throughout the book, you'll know to use your **detective equipment** in the activity.

💻 When you see this symbol throughout the book, you'll know there's a related activity to be found on the Detective Academy **website**.

Case File

Welcome to Detective Academy!

Do you feel the need to finish a puzzle when you start it? Do you notice details other people miss—like a friend's new haircut or a change in your neighborhood (maybe a house got a paint job or a new street sign went up)? If you've already got great observation skills and a drive to solve puzzles, problems, or mysteries, you're on your way to becoming a great **detective**!

As a Detective Academy **rookie**, you'll learn how to pick up on tiny details that help make sharp detectives. You'll explore the world of **crime scene** investigation, learn how to collect **evidence**, practice taking fingerprints from any type of surface, and figure out who is likely to be guilty of committing a crime. You'll also learn how to exercise your memory so it's razor-sharp, and how to interview **witnesses** and potential **suspects**.

*See if you can *detect* the **boldface** words throughout the book. Check out what these words mean in the *Detective Jargon* section on page 12.

ABOUT THIS BOOK

This *Basic Training Manual* is where you start. It's the beginning of your course of study at Detective Academy. You'll earn your detective **credentials** (your **shield** and ID card), start an official investigations notebook, learn how to use detective gadgets, and much more. You'll also get the inside track on behind-the-scenes detective work and find out all about real-life crimes that detectives have solved. Plus, you'll find stories of real detectives that will help inspire you when working on your own investigations. And you'll learn all this from real detectives! Then, each month after this, for as long as you're a Detective Academy rookie, you'll get another book that focuses in detail on one area of detective work, along with another kit of detective equipment.

CASE FILES

The case files are the activities and challenges you'll find in each book throughout Detective Academy. As you try your hand at cracking, or solving, cases, you'll be the *lead investigator*—interviewing witnesses, combing crime scenes for clues...putting your new detective skills to work!

THE REAL DEAL

The skills that you practice in the case files are the *real skills* that detectives need and use every day. They're powerful tools; they help detectives find the person or people that they're looking for...the ones who are *guilty* of a crime.

So if you're prepared to keep your eyes and ears open, to think about what you see and hear, and to look beyond the obvious, then you've come to the right place—Detective Academy—to start your journey toward becoming a great detective!

P.S. As you work on your activities throughout this book, check out *Case Closed* on pages 47–48 for answers.

Detective Equipment

While your best asset as a detective is your mind—the more you use it, the better—every detective also needs some special equipment. Here's what you get this month:

- A **detective shield and shield case**, which, along with your **ID card**, are your credentials. You'll have these with you when you're working a crime scene or interviewing witnesses.

- A **flashlight** for use at night or if you're searching for clues in dark places.

- A **high-powered magnifying glass (magnified 10x)** so you can examine tiny clues such as **trace evidence**.

- An **investigations notebook and pencil** to keep track of clues you need to solve cases.

- A **detective equipment case** so you can bring your tools of the trade with you to crime scenes. It comes complete with a belt loop so you can carry it easily with you.

Detective Academy Website

Want more ways to practice your skills as a detective? Then get online at **www.scholastic.com/detective**. The website card included in your detective equipment kit provides your first password so you can log on. This month's password is **rookie**. Each month you'll get another password to gain access to the next site. You'll find the password in each upcoming Detective Academy book.

Dear Detective Rookie,

Welcome to Detective Academy™! You're new to the force, your work shift has just begun, and it's time for Roll Call. If you're here, please sign in by reporting to the Detective Academy website at **www.scholastic.com/detective**. That's where you'll get your credentials: your shield number for your shield and ID card.

You'll need to have your password handy to get past the station house entrance. It is:

PASSWORD: rookie

Once you're on the website, you'll be able to:
- Sharpen your observation skills
- Challenge yourself to solve mysteries inspired by real-life cases
- Create IDs so your friends can join your detective squad

PASSWORD: rookie

5

The Lowdown on Detectives

When people think of the police, they usually think of the police officer on the corner who keeps the neighborhood safe, or who drives around in a police car with flashing lights and sirens. It's pretty easy to spot these officers—they wear uniforms and display badges, which set them apart from the crowd. They're tough to miss—and that's on purpose (*criminals* can see them just as easily as you can, and reconsider their plans for the day—which is a way of stopping crimes *before* they happen).

Detectives, on the other hand, are *plainclothes* police officers, which means they usually don't wear uniforms. Generally, detectives wear business suits when they work, or they might "dress down" (just like how you wear school clothes or play clothes, depending on what you're going out to do). Either way, the key is that a detective working a case usually just *looks* like your average businessman or businesswoman...until the case is solved and the handcuffs come out!

Police officers and detectives work closely together, but their jobs are very different. For instance, when a crime has occurred and you call 911, it's police officers (not detectives) who come to help you. If, when they arrive, these officers see someone committing a crime, they'll arrest him on the spot.

Detectives, on the other hand, are called in *after* a crime has been committed. What detectives spend their time doing is looking for clues and talking to people. They're trying to re-create the past in their heads, to figure out exactly what happened, who did it, and where that person is now.

Hit the Road: Unmarked (Detective) Cars vs. Marked (Police) Cars

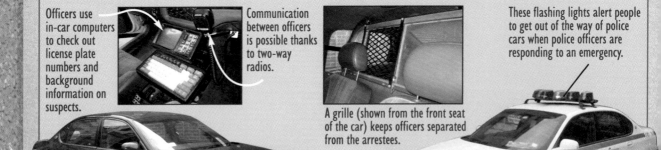

Officers use in-car computers to check out license plate numbers and background information on suspects.

Communication between officers is possible thanks to two-way radios.

These flashing lights alert people to get out of the way of police cars when police officers are responding to an emergency.

A grille (shown from the front seat of the car) keeps officers separated from the arrestees.

Detectives drive special unmarked cars like the one shown here. An unmarked car doesn't have the markings of a police car.

These headlights conceal flashing lights like the ones you can see on the top of marked police cars.

Uniformed police officers drive marked police cars like this one. A marked car is clearly identified as a police car.

With every crime, there is one detective who is "assigned" to the case—he's responsible for solving it, he's the *lead investigator*. He doesn't solve the crime all by himself, however. A detective working the case is like a movie director, instructing the police officers at the **crime scene**, bringing in other detectives with special skills to help him, and planning the whole investigation.

In order to solve a crime, a detective might have to visit a lot of people and places. So to prove who they are, detectives carry **shields** and ID cards (just like police officers—and just like the ones you got in your equipment kit!), but they

Police Department Family Tree: Detectives and Patrol

Police Chief (or Chief of Police)

Chief of Detectives — Chief of Patrol

District Commanders (Captain) — Precinct Commanders (Captain)

Squad Supervisors (Detective Lieutenants or Detective Sergeants) — Lieutenant — Lieutenant

Detectives — Sergeant — Sergeant — Sergeant

Police Officers

Detectives work in detective squads (or groups) that are separate from police officers. They answer to special supervisors, either detective **sergeants** or detective **lieutenants**. The person who's in charge of the detective squad is called the chief of detectives.

usually keep them in a pocket or wear them around their necks on a chain. A detective working a case can display his shield when he wants his identity to be known—at a crime scene, for instance, or when talking to a **witness** or **eyewitness**. Like police officers, detectives also carry guns, since their work can be dangerous at times—but detectives keep theirs out of sight. Detectives carry other equipment, too, like flashlights, cell phones, radios, pagers, notebooks, and containers for collecting **evidence**. You may have noticed that you, too, have a lot of stuff in your Detective Academy equipment kit!

Detective [ke] Glynn

Police Officer Debra Gosset

Belt pouch holds handcuffs.

Handcuffs and a detective shield.

A cell phone (or pager) helps detectives communicate.

Mace (a type of spray that stings your eyes) is carried by an officer in case she has to deal with a dangerous person.

A flashlight.

A radio for communication.

A chemical mask in case of terrorist attack.

7

DOWN AT HEADQUARTERS

Detectives have their offices in police stations—usually on the second floor or in a separate wing from regular police officers. This is their home base, where they keep all their files and work their cases. Of course, detectives are often out of the office working crime scenes or interviewing witnesses. Detectives have to be able to go all over town to search for clues *and* for criminals. Sometimes they might even have to go to a different town or city to find some clue or someone. Some detectives are even sent to other countries when the **suspects** they're looking for flee.

Police departments can be large or small, depending on how big an area they cover. A small town might have a very small police department. It might be so small that there's only one detective. That detective is going to have to be especially smart and resourceful so he can solve cases all by himself!

A Cutaway Floorplan of a Police Station in Action

INTERROGATION ROOM

Detectives interview witnesses and interrogate suspects in this private room (unless you're a detective, you don't want to be here!).

PRECINCT GYM

While there's no fitness requirement, uniformed officers and detectives are encouraged to exercise in order to remain fit. They often exercise on their lunch breaks, before eating. Because criminals work out, too, it pays to be prepared!

CLERICAL OFFICE

Employees work here to help uniformed officers and detectives with paperwork—otherwise, detectives and police officers could get buried beneath all those forms and reports!

THE DESK

The "Desk Officer" (usually a lieutenant or sergeant) sits here and makes sure that a new prisoner's arrest is handled correctly. The D.O. is also responsible for supervising the whole precinct. He's sort of like a lunchroom monitor with a badge!

BAR FOR HANDCUFFING

A prisoner is handcuffed at the Desk while his arrest forms are being filled out. This ensures that the perpetrator doesn't go for a neighborhood stroll while the police officer fills out an arrest report!

ONE-WAY MIRROR

A one-way mirror is see-through on one side and looks like a regular mirror on the other. That way, the victim or witness can identify the suspect in a lineup without themselves being seen by the suspect.

DETECTIVE LIEUTENANT'S OFFICE

The lieutenant—who's in charge of the detectives at this precinct—has his office here, near the rest of the detectives. The lieutenant is usually a very experienced detective who has handled many different cases.

LINEUP WALL

To see if detectives have the right suspect, they sometimes do a lineup with five other similar-looking people. The witness or victim of the crime (behind the one-way mirror) has to pick the correct suspect out of the group.

DETECTIVES' OFFICES

Detectives work here when they're not out interviewing witnesses or suspects, or searching crime scenes. They do research, work on their reports, and drink enough coffee every day to fill a bathtub!

HOLDING CELL

A prisoner is held here after he's arrested—until he goes before a judge in a court of law to be formally "booked" for a crime.

LOCKERS

Where can detectives store all their stuff? In lockers—just like the ones you have at school!

RECEPTION AREA

This is where you would go to report a complaint (no, not that you have too much homework or that your new jeans don't fit—a complaint of a crime, like that your bicycle was stolen. Unfortunately, detectives don't help with homework!).

POLICE STATION ENTRANCE

WORKING THE CASE

So how *does* a detective begin working her magic? Let's start at the beginning, shall we?

After a crime has been committed, a detective is called in to "work the case," which is police talk for figuring out what happened. Just like in a school cafeteria lunch line, detectives take turns working cases—whoever's up next "catches" the next case (that is, gets assigned to it). When a detective catches a new case, she usually starts working at the place where the crime occurred—the crime scene. That's where the detective is likely to find the most clues. At a crime scene, some clues are found in evidence that must be collected and analyzed.

So you've caught a case—now what? Well, that's tough to say—every day in a detective's life is different! Usually, a detective working a case will start at the crime scene—but after that, it's anybody's guess. She might be out interviewing witnesses, "tailing" (following) a suspect, or "sitting on" (watching) a suspect's house. Or she might be back at her office, making phone calls to check into a suspect's background or filling out the paperwork that goes with every case (yes, detectives have homework, too!). Either way, she's using all the evidence to narrow down her list of suspects...until it's narrowed down to the real perpetrator (or perpetrators). Then, the case is solved!

THE NIGHT SHIFT

Uniformed police officers work "around the clock"—that is, 24 hours a day, 7 days a week, every day of the year (criminals don't exactly keep normal business hours, you know!). But police officers can't work *all the time*—they need to go home to be with their families, and to sleep, just like you do, so their day is divided up into shifts. There are police officers who work during the daytime (from 8 a.m. until 4 p.m.), in the evening (from 4 p.m. until midnight), and overnight (from midnight until 8 a.m.).

Detectives keep a similar schedule, but unlike uniformed police officers, they might need to work during the morning one day and at night the next. For instance, let's say a detective goes to investigate a stolen car during the day. That night, she might want to drive around

detective!

This is a 24-hour clock to go with 24-hour shifts!

town to see if someone—a suspect—parked the stolen car near his house. For that reason, detective shifts rotate. A detective might work two evening shifts in a row, then two during the day, then get a couple of days off (this can be tough on sleeping habits—imagine trying to go to bed at 8 a.m.!).

The New Canaan, Connecticut, police station.

Whatever shift they work, detectives sometimes use specialists to help them collect evidence at crime scenes. **Crime Scene Investigation (CSI) technicians** are people who are specifically trained to collect and handle evidence—making sure it isn't disturbed or tampered with. Sometimes, the evidence collected goes to **forensic scientists** (scientists who analyze small or even microscopic clues, such as fingerprints and cloth fibers). Like any project, it's good to have friends to help out! A top-notch detective will listen carefully to what the CSI technicians and forensic scientists have to say.

In some small police departments—in small towns or country areas—a single detective might have to take on all of these specialized roles (imagine having the *same* teacher for math, science, English, social studies, *and* gym, and you'll get the idea). That detective has to be highly skilled and trained (he also has to live without much sleep!). On big cases, small-town detectives might ask for help from a nearby city, or even from the Federal Bureau of Investigation (or the FBI—more on them on page 26). Do you know some *other* **rookie** detectives who'll be able to help *you* out when you're working a crime scene?

WHAT'S IT TAKE?

So what does it take to become a detective? You can't just walk down to the local precinct and sign up—you need some training and experience first! That's why all detectives start their careers as police officers. Everyone who enters police work in the U.S. must be at least 21 years old, a citizen, and a high school graduate—a college degree is helpful, too. (You can never know too much as a detective!) And detectives all have one thing in common: They use their brainpower to snatch suspects who thought they "got away with it."

The 10th police precinct in New York City, New York.

Once on the force, all rookie police officers go through a training program in topics like law, use of firearms, self-defense, and first aid. After that, they are assigned to work in uniform, on patrol (meaning they "patrol" the streets, protecting people and preventing crime). A patrol officer must then establish his arrest credentials (meaning he has to make enough arrests to gain experience). Finally, a detective hopeful gets to spend a little over a year with experienced investigators who can teach him the tricks of the trade. If he makes the grade, he's promoted and becomes a full-fledged detective!

Here are some words you'll see in **boldface** throughout the book to get you talking like a real detective!

Credentials: Proof that you really are a detective, like your shield or ID card.

Crime Scene: This is usually the actual location of a crime, but it can also be the area where the crime was planned or the entry point where the criminal got into the place where he committed the crime.

Crime Scene Investigation (CSI) Technician: Someone who helps a detective find and preserve evidence at a crime scene. Unlike the detective, a CSI technician is not responsible for solving a crime, but rather for analyzing clues found at a crime scene. He then gives that analysis over to the detective for her to solve the crime.

Detective: A person who investigates and is responsible for putting all the pieces together to solve a crime.

Evidence: Anything that might help solve a crime, like an article of clothing left at the scene of a robbery or a ransom note left at the scene of a kidnapping.

Eyewitness: A person who saw a crime with their own eyes, like a pedestrian who saw two cars collide.

First Responder: The first officer at the scene of a crime—usually a uniformed patrol officer who got the information on an emergency from the dispatcher.

Forensic Scientist: Scientists who analyze small or even microscopic clues, like fingerprints and cloth fibers.

Lieutenant: A rank of police officer or detective that is two levels above a new police officer and one above a sergeant.

Motive: The reason why a person does something, like committing a crime.

Perpetrator: Person who commits a crime (sometimes abbreviated as *perp*).

Precinct: The neighborhood that a particular police station is assigned to keep safe.

Rookie: Someone who is just getting started on their training—in this case a rookie police officer or detective.

Sergeant: A police ranking that is one level higher than a new police officer.

Shield: A badge that helps prove a detective's credentials.

Suspect: A person who may have committed a crime, who might be the perpetrator.

Trace Evidence: Tiny pieces of evidence, like hair, fiber, and dust, that you might find to help you solve the crime.

Victim: A person who is hurt—whether they're physically hurt or hurt because something was stolen from them—as a result of a perpetrator.

Witness: A person who knows something about a crime, even though he may not have actually seen the crime happen.

What Happened Here...and Who Did It?

All **detectives** need excellent observation skills. A detective's ability to look at a room and observe clues is what sets him apart from someone who looks at a room and sees...a room.

It's time to start your **rookie** training in real detective skills. Take a look at the picture below. Do you see anything out of place? Only *time* will tell if you can pinpoint all the evidence. Here's another hint: How would a *person* open a bag of trail mix like the one below? It's all a bit *nuts*, don't you think? Take your time—there's more going on here than your eyes might first see! And remember the two questions you're trying to answer, just like any detective:

- *What happened here?*
- *Who did it?*

Oh, and one last hint: Your magnifying glass from your equipment kit might come in handy!

Check out *Case Closed* at the end of the book to find out how you did!

Trained Eyes

Stuff You'll Need
• Notebook (DA)
• Pencil (DA)
• A friend
• A timer or watch

Now that you've warmed up your observation skills, it's time to take a *closer* look at your surroundings. Observation is a key part of an investigation. When a **detective** observes a **crime scene**, he "takes in" the scene. Taking in a scene means examining the obvious clues, but it also means noticing the *not-so-obvious* ones. Detectives have to be what are called "trained observers."

The place where a crime occurred has a story to tell. In a way, the crime scene is like a big jigsaw puzzle that hasn't yet been put together. Pieces of the puzzle are lying around, right in front of your eyes. Some are stuck under other pieces and some are turned upside down. With a little patience and a lot of detective work, each of the pieces will fit together to make a picture—enough for you to solve the crime.

What You Do

Part I. New Eyes

In this activity, you're going to take a look at your room as if you were seeing it for the first time, just like a detective does when approaching a crime scene. Your room would reveal a lot about you to a stranger, don't you think?

1. Go into your room as though you were a detective who has never been there before. Pretend that it isn't your room—you're seeing it the way a detective, new to the scene, would observe it. Take time to really look at your surroundings.

2. According to what you see in your room, what were you likely to have been doing last? Reading? (Is there an open book on your bed?) Homework? (Are there pages of a book report scattered about?) Playing a video game? (Forgot to turn it off again?) Eating? (Potato chips, anyone?) Chilling out on the bed? (Is your bedspread rumpled?)

3. What does your room say about what you like to do? Is there sports stuff lying around—cluing in an observer to the fact that you're an athlete? Is there a collection of comic books in your room? What kinds of pictures or posters are decorating your walls? Could a detective tell that you love music or that you're a soccer fan?

4. Does anything in your room tell an observer about your family? Maybe you've got twin siblings and there are pictures of them in your room? Are you in the photos, too? If so, what's the expression on your face? Could a detective tell anything about your relationship to your siblings from the photo? You *do* get along with your brothers and sisters, don't you?

5. In your notebook, make a list of your observations with your "new" eyes. Did you notice how obvious it is that you love soccer? Or how you tend to collect things like a pack rat?

Check out this 10-year-old's bedroom. Then look at the same picture below. Can you spot the *five* things that have been moved around? Look in *Case Closed* to see if you're right!

Part II. Change of Scenery

Now that you've explored your room like never before, see if you can tell when your stuff's been messed with!

1. Invite a fellow **rookie** to make a few small changes in your room— nothing too obvious—while you wait in another room for a few minutes. He might open a book, rearrange your music collection, or eat some chips and leave crumbs on your desk.

2. When he's finished, go into your room and try to see what's different. How long does it take you to spot the changes? Do you notice them all? Check with your fellow rookie to see if you're right.

3. Next time you go to your training partner's house, switch roles: *You* change something in *his* room and see if he can figure it out.

Part III. The Room...Speaks!

Now that you've trained your eyes to "read" a room, let's see if you can make a room talk! For this activity, imagine you're trying to point out who the **perpetrator** of a crime is— without saying a single word.

1. First, have your fellow rookie leave the room. Before he comes back, your goal is to provide him with enough clues to lead him to the guilty party. Think you can manage it without blurting out the answer? You'll need a bit of setup first. So, with the permission of a senior detective, gather together whatever materials you think you'll need to indicate that instead of *you*, one of the following **suspects** lives in your room:

    - An athlete
    - A bookworm
    - A cook
    - A musician
    - A person of your choice

2. Now, ask yourself: What clues can I give that indicate one of these people lives here? What stuff would this person leave lying around? Before your fellow rookie comes back, write down each suspect on a separate piece of paper and leave each paper on your bed.

3. Let your partner back in the room. Then point out that you've laid out the five pieces of paper with the suspect choices on your bed. Tell him: "The person who inhabits this room is guilty of a crime. You have one minute to figure out which of these suspects did it." Oh! And one more thing: *All your clues have to be visible.* That is, all the stuff you've chosen must be in plain sight.

4. If he guesses right, your partner should be able to list every clue you left him. If he misses some, that's okay; but if he doesn't, that's even better!

5. When you're done, reverse roles. You can also come up with different possible suspects. For instance: How would you indicate that a *detective* lives in your room? Think about it!

What's the Real Deal?

The things in your room paint a pretty good picture of who you are. Imagine you're trying to find your best friend to go to the park with. You go to his house, but he isn't there. You probably have a pretty good idea where he might be (already at the park or maybe at the mall instead). When a detective is searching for someone, he has to get to know him as well as you know your best friend. That person's room is a great place to start.

When your fellow rookie moved stuff around in your room, were you surprised at how long it took you to find the changes? Or did your excellent detective eyes spot them right away? A detective coming to a crime scene won't have the benefit of studying the scene *before* the crime occurred (like you did before your friend made some changes). Still, he's got to be able to notice what's out of place—or what seems like it shouldn't be there.

Remember: Every crime scene *wants* to speak to you. If you can learn to make one speak yourself, you're halfway to hearing what *any* crime scene has to say.

IDentify Yourself

Now that you've gotten yourself warmed up as a sharp-eyed **detective**, it's time to get your **credentials**! You'll need them when you're working a case—at a **crime scene** or interviewing **witnesses**.

Every detective has an ID card and a **shield**, and every shield has a number. The number is a quick way that a detective can identify himself to his fellow detectives on the job. Shield numbers are assigned to new recruits in sequential order when they join the force (meaning that if a new recruit signs up and the next available number is 237, then that's her number). In a large police department, with thousands of detectives, the shield numbers get pretty high. In a tiny detective squad with just five detectives, the shield numbers would only go up to five!

Normally, it isn't up to a detective what his shield number is. The detective squad assigns him a number and that's that. But detectives become pretty attached to their numbers—so attached, in fact, that when a new detective is the son or daughter of a retired detective, the squad allows the retiree to hand down his shield and number to his child so that the number stays in the family.

Detectives are required to keep their shields with them at all times. If they're off-duty and witness a crime, they've got to take action! When they do, they'll need their shield to prove who they are. So, **rookie**, always carry your shield—in your pocket or around your neck.

Stuff You'll Need

- Pen
- Slip of paper for your shield number (found in your equipment kit in the same pack as the notebook) DA
- Shield DA
- Shield case DA
- ID card DA
- Photo of yourself that you can cut to size
- Scissors
- Ruler
- Glue or tape

What You Do

Part I. The Shield

1. Log on to the Detective Academy website at **www.scholastic.com/detective** to get your shield number. The Shield Number Generator will give you your own personal shield number that will be yours as a member of Detective Academy! If you prefer, you can come up with your own number—maybe one that has some meaning to you (like your birthday or the age of your pets).

2. Once you've got your shield number, write it down on the piece of paper (the really small one) that came with your Detective Academy shield.

3. Slip the shield number into the slot on the side of the shield (make sure the shield number is facing out). Tear off the extra bit of paper.

27983

17

Part II. ID Me!

1. To accompany your shield, you need an ID card that identifies you as a detective. Take the card out of your equipment kit and fill it in! Write down the shield number you created in *Part I*. Then fill in the rest of the details: your name, your age, your height and weight. Don't forget to sign the card!

2. Now take a photo of yourself that you can cut (get the permission of a senior detective first!). Cut out the picture so it's 1 x 1 inches square. Then glue or tape the photo to your ID card where it says "Place photo here."

3. Slide your new official Detective Academy ID card into the plastic slot on the back of your shield case. Wear your shield and ID card whenever you're out working on a case or doing your detective training. Remember to keep it with you at all times!

More From Detective Squad

Make a couple of extra IDs for your friends or fellow detective rookies. You can go to the Detective Academy website (**www.scholastic.com/detective**) and print out more IDs. Or, if you prefer, you can make ID cards from paper and colored pens or pencils.

What's the Real Deal?

When a police officer is promoted to detective, it's quite a big deal! The police department has a ceremony and all the new detectives bring their families to celebrate—almost like graduation day at school. Each detective walks up on a stage and is presented with his new detective shield by the chief of police and the chief of detectives. After the ceremony, each detective sits for a photo, which is then put on his new ID card to go with his new shield.

Here are a few different types of detective shields and patches. Notice anything different from your shield? These shields don't have numbers! Once you get promoted to a "boss"—a detective **sergeant** or **lieutenant**—you don't need a shield number anymore...you're unique enough!

As small As the Eye Can See

Stuff You'll Need

- 5 objects in a room
- A cloth
- A friend
- Magnifying glass

Now that you've got your **credentials** together, it's time to get back to *focusing* on your observation skills! Wondering what the best way to do that is? The answer's at the *tip* of your fingers!

Fingerprints are patterns on your fingers made up of friction ridges. When you touch something, the oils on your skin come off in the shape of that pattern—leaving a fingerprint behind. If you hold your index finger up to the light, you can see those ridges. Go up to a mirror and press your thumb on the glass. See the oval impression it makes? If you were a criminal and you accidentally left a print like that at a **crime scene**, the responding **detectives** would have the case halfway solved. The reason the case would be only *halfway* solved is that the criminal's fingerprints would have to already be on *file*. When a person gets arrested, police take his fingerprints. One reason is so that if he ever commits another crime and leaves fingerprints at the scene, detectives can easily identify who he is. When fingerprints are found at a crime scene and no matches are on file, detectives must find other ways to identify the criminal. Once they do, his fingerprints can be compared to those they found at the crime scene. Some cases aren't solved until years later, when the criminal is arrested for a different crime and is fingerprinted for the first time and the match is made!

What You Do

Part I. Sticky Fingers

How good are you at spotting fingerprints? Invite a friend over and see how easily (or not) you can find his prints on your stuff!

1. Pick five different objects—such as a TV screen, a picture frame, a mirror, a computer screen, and a window—in a room, like your family room, and wipe them clean with a cloth. Make sure you don't leave any of your own fingerprints behind.

2. While you wait in the hallway, have your friend go into the room and touch two of the five objects. Make sure you tell him

If this were *your* family room, which five objects would you choose to have your friend leave his fingerprints on? (There are more than five good surfaces pictured.)

what the five objects are first, but don't let him tell you the two he'll be leaving his prints on—after all, criminals are never that cooperative!

3. When your friend is done, go into the room with your magnifying glass. Carefully inspect each of the five objects until you find the two he put his hands on.

4. Switch roles and have him try to find your fingerprints!

Part II. Trace It Back

Fingerprints aren't the only microscopic clues that criminals unintentionally leave at crime scenes. Trace evidence is evidence so small that it often needs to be looked at up close under a microscope or with a magnifying glass. Get up close with your carpet or rug to see what unwelcome outsiders have made themselves at home in your house!

1. Got any shaggy carpets? Use your magnifying glass to take a closer look.

Spread apart the fibers of the carpet and inspect it at its base.

2. If your carpet is green, do you notice any fibers of a different color, like red or blue, that shouldn't be there?

3. See any specks of dirt or dog hair that have made themselves comfortable in your rug? Any crumbs from last week's pizza?

More From Detective Squad

Think you're getting good at spotting tiny details? Have you noticed any so far in this book? Go back and take another look...with your magnifying glass! There are *nine* words hidden throughout the book. Once you find them all, unscramble them to discover a hidden message. To get started, take a close look at this page with your magnifying glass. Check out *Case Closed* for the answer!

CASE IN POINT Perfect Print

In November 1999, a man named Cazzie L. Williams walked into a bank in Paramus, NJ, and handed the teller a note that read,

You Have Less Than 2 Minutes to Give Me All the $100 Dollar Bills and All of the $50 Dollar Bills From This Register!!! Don't Be Stupid Because Someone's Life Could Be in Your Hands!!!

In addition to the instructions, Williams left something else on the note, and in the bank itself: his fingerprints! Even though Williams's prints were on file in another part of the country, it took three years for detectives to realize that, match the prints, and then catch up with Williams. But when they finally *did* catch him and show him the evidence, he confessed—and not just to the bank robbery in Paramus, but to 26 other holdups since 1997, and to making off with more than $100,000 in loot!

What's the Real Deal?

Crime Scene Investigation (CSI) technicians are experts in finding tiny pieces of evidence in unlikely places, but the ultimate responsibility for the case isn't theirs—it's the investigating detective's. For that reason, every detective must work to become good at examining crime scenes, and must accompany the CSI technicians as they remove and safeguard evidence. Remember, the detective is like the director, and just because one actor, like a crime scene tech (short for technician), may know his part, the director must still direct! Also, like a movie set, it's very important that the crime scene not be disturbed. You saw in your carpet or rug how tiny evidence can be and how easily it's inadvertently brought into a crime scene. The dirt a criminal tracks in is excellent evidence, but a detective must make sure that one of the crime scene techs, police officers, or **first responders** didn't track in the dirt themselves (like the detective munching on the sandwich in this picture!). When you come to a crime scene, you have to make sure that no one's there who shouldn't be. And when you find evidence, you must always think to yourself, *Did the criminal leave that, or did I?*

Ever wonder how a magnifying glass works? When you look at something with your naked eyes, what you see is actually the light reflected off of what you're looking at. That's why you need to turn on the lights in a dark room to read a book. See how the lens of your magnifying glass is a little curved toward the center? The light reflected off what you're looking at enters the curved lens and is spread out. That way, reflections that are very close together—like the letters from this tiny print—look wider and taller, and can be read.

Some magnifying glasses are more powerful than others. When a magnifying glass is listed as being "5x," that means it increases the size of an object to five times its original size (at least, that's how your eye sees it—it doesn't really grow!). But magnifying glasses can be much stronger than that, like 10x, 20x, or even 50x. And if you really need to see something up close, you can put it under a microscope. This can increase the size that you see an object by 1000x, in some cases. Unfortunately, microscopes don't exactly fit in a detective's back pocket!

Detectives carry magnifying glasses like the ones shown here with them to crime scenes. The large one, at left, has 5x magnification power and the smaller one, at right, has 3x power. (The one in your equipment kit has 10x magnification.)

Can you use *your* magnifying glass to read the mini text in these two magnifying glasses?

Magnification
Investigation

Now that you've been honing your observation skills in the last few case files, put them to the test with some real-life **evidence**. When a **detective** searches a **crime scene**, he could turn up lots of fingerprints. Great, right? Maybe, but not all fingerprints can be used. A detective needs to be able to compare the prints he finds at the crime scene with those of the **suspect**. In order to do so, he needs to get a *clean* print. What does that mean? The ridges on a person's finger form shapes called loops and whorls (sort of like the marks that wet sneakers leave on a dry sidewalk). If these ridges don't come up clean—meaning they're smudged, too faint to read, or don't have any visible ridges at all—the detective won't be able to tell if the suspect's fingerprints match.

What You Do

Part I. Separating the Good From the Bad

1. Have a look at the fingerprints here that were found on a cash box at a recent robbery. Get out your magnifying glass and study them carefully. Can you see those ridges we were just talking about? On all of the prints or just some of them?

2. Circle the prints you think are *clean*. Remember, there should be visible ridges—no smudged or faint prints, and no prints without ridges at all. Check out *Case Closed* to see how you did.

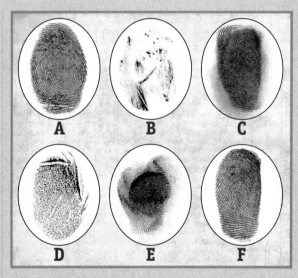

A   B   C

D   E   F

Part II. Location, Location!

One of the factors that determines the quality of a fingerprint—whether it's *clean*—is the surface that it's found on. Remember in *Case File #3: As Small As the Eye Can See* when your friend put his fingerprints on a glass surface like a mirror or window? Glass is one of the easiest places to get good prints because it's hard and smooth. But what about other surfaces?

1. Get a dollar bill. (If you need to, borrow one from a senior detective. Remember to give it back, though!) Press your finger onto it and try to leave a fingerprint. Have a look with your magnifying glass.

Do you see anything? Fingerprints are really hard to find on money because money is soft and textured, although they can be found *sometimes*!

2. Look around your house and see what other surfaces you think might be good for finding fingerprints. Which surfaces might not be so good? How about the refrigerator? The TV? A wooden door? A curtain? Remember what traits make for good prints!

This small magnifier contains a light below the lens—perfect for studying prints in the dark.

What's the Real Deal?

Getting a clean print is crucial to identifying a suspect. In fact, if the right loops and whorls are clear, sometimes even a *partial* print can be enough to ID the **perpetrator**!

Looking around your house for places where fingerprints might be found is very much like what detectives do at real crime scenes. You can't examine every single surface at a crime scene—that could take a week! Detectives need to know what surfaces are likely to have fingerprints on them, so that they can concentrate their efforts on searching that part of the crime scene, instead of wasting valuable time when the criminal could be getting away!

CASE IN POINT
First Fingerprints

In 1904, New York Police Department (NYPD) detective Sergeant Joseph Faurot was sent to England to learn how to use fingerprints to catch criminals. At that time, the European detectives were more advanced than American ones in the use of scientific methods of fighting crime. Faurot returned to New York to teach his fellow detectives the new techniques, but it took a while for fingerprinting to become widely accepted. It wasn't until there was a burglary at the fancy Waldorf-Astoria hotel in New York—where a thief stole jewelry and other valuables from guests—that other detectives really began to take notice of the importance of fingerprints. Faurot was able to identify the prints left at the scene as belonging to an international hotel jewelry thief. Coincidentally, the information about the thief was provided by Scotland Yard, the detective squad in England, since the criminal already had stolen there!

The Waldorf-Astoria back in the early 1900s.

You Saw What?

You saw how important it is to really use your eyes at a **crime scene** in *Case File #1: Trained Eyes*, among others—there's nothing more important than your powers of observation when working a case. Fingerprints and other **evidence** at the scene can very often tell you what you need to know. Want to know where *else* you can get important details about a crime? From other people!

Witnesses are people who have seen something important related to a crime—sometimes the crime itself, sometimes the **perpetrator** fleeing the scene, sometimes a tiny detail that they didn't think was important...until a **detective** showed up and started asking the right questions.

That's why, as a detective, you've got to know the right questions to ask. Here are the big "Six Questions":

- **Who?** Who am I talking to? What's his name? His address? His phone number? His job?
- **What?** What is he telling me? What did he see? Is it important?
- **Where?** Where was he when he saw what he saw? How far away was he?
- **When?** What time was it when he saw what he saw? What time (or day) is it now? How long ago did he see what he's describing?
- **Why?** Why did this person see all this? Why was the crime committed? And why is this person talking to me? Is he a witness, or was he involved in the crime?
- **How?** How did the crime happen?

What You Do

Part I. Jot Down the Facts

Interviewing a witness is a very important detective skill, so, **rookie**, you might as well get started developing your technique. You're a detective investigating a bank robbery. You're back at your office interviewing witnesses. An 18-year-old woman named Brittany Jones is brought in. As soon as she sits down, she begins talking. And talking, and talking, and talking. You decide to let her continue, rather than interrupt her (an excellent interview technique, by the way).

1. *So I was, like, you know, going to the bank this morning, and it's, like, really crowded, you know? I'm, like, waiting on this line, and then these guys just, like, barge into the bank. There were, like, two or three of them or something, and then*

they started yelling that it was a bank robbery, you know, like, "Everybody be quiet! Give us the money!" or something like that, like they think they're on TV! These guys were all wearing the same clothes, like, they all had white shirts and black pants, and brown shoes. And then one of them—the shortest one, who was, like, the size of my little brother, like, 5' 2"—starts waving this gun around like he's in a movie, like he thinks he's cool, and then this other guy, this big, like, Incredible Hulk guy, says, "Put all the money in the bag!" and the bank people gave him all this money, and he put it in the sack, and then they left. They got in this car that was, like, totally lame—this green color. So that's, like, what I saw.

2. Yikes! Still want to be a detective? Believe it or not, Brittany is *not* a bad witness. Yes, she's a bit chatty (well, maybe more than just a *bit*) and she's told you some things that have nothing to do with the case—but she's told you some important things, too. It's *your* job to figure out what's important and what's not. So go back through Brittany's statement and, using your pencil, underline the parts that you think are important to your case. With Brittany's help, you've just begun to put together some answers to the "Six Questions" of this crime.

Part II. Attention, Please!

After Brittany leaves, another witness is brought in by one of your fellow detectives who's helping with the case (remember, other detectives might help out on the case, but

JUST THE FACTS

Detectives have to keep their notes along with the case file for when they testify at trial. Trials sometimes start long after the case is solved and the detective may need his notes to refresh his memory of the details of the case.

you are the *lead investigator*). This time, the witness is a man, 51 years old. Here's what he tells you:

1. My name's Al Smith. I own Smith Garage, across the street from that bank that got robbed today. It was about 9:45, maybe a little later, I'm not sure. I was working on this pickup truck a guy brought in with a flat. All of a sudden I heard some shouting from across the street, so I looked up from the tire and I saw two guys with masks run out of the bank and get into a green Volkswagen Bug and drive away real fast. They were both wearing black pants and white shirts and work boots, pretty much like the ones I wear.

> Describe 3 perps:
> #1/ B/m , 20 to 25 yrs. 6'00", 160 lbs, Scar on left cheek. Blue jacket Blue pants, Green BB cap.
> #2/ w/m , 15 to 18 yrs, 5'7", 140 lbs, Brn. hair very short, jean jacket
> #3/ H/m , 15 to 18 yrs 5'10", 180 lbs, Brn hair short, overweight, bandana on head - red, white T-shirt Blue pants.

These actual notes from a detective's notebook show what important info he jots down and the way he abbreviates certain words—can you figure out what each abbreviation means? Check out *Case Closed* to see if you're right.

Part III. Mixing and Matching

Mr. Smith was a good witness, too. He confirmed some of Brittany's details, and added a few significant ones of his own. Did you pick up on them?

25

1. Now it's time to see what you've learned. You've got two pretty good witnesses who saw the crime from two different angles. Look at the case report below (based on a real police department form). How much of it can you fill in to start getting a picture of who you're looking for? Check out *Case Closed.*

Case Report	Detective's Name and Shield Number:
Today's Date:	**Crime:**
Location (this is the *Where*):	
Time of Occurrence (this is the *When*):	
Method of Crime (this is the *What* and *How*—describe what you believe happened):	
Perpetrators/Suspects (this is the *Who*):	
Names of Witnesses (this is also the *Who*):	
Property Taken (this is the *What* and the *Why*. What was stolen? If nothing, then why was the crime committed? What was the motive?):	
Case Status (circle one): **Open** **Closed by Arrest**	

SPOTLIGHT ON

THE FBI

Just like you sometimes need help with your homework, detectives sometimes need help on cases. The Federal Bureau of Investigation (FBI) is the nation's premier law enforcement agency that has the best crime lab, forensic scientists, and general training of any agency in the world. And, they're available to help detectives with some of their cases, such as bank robberies. The FBI calls its investigators "Special Agents," and they have the responsibility to enforce federal laws—laws that cover the whole country (bank robbery is against both state and federal laws).

What's the Real Deal?

When a serious crime occurs—and a bank robbery is definitely a serious crime—there can be an awful lot of witnesses. Imagine if the bank was crowded when it was robbed and the robbers escaped into rush hour traffic. You'd have to interview everyone in the bank and everyone who might have seen the bank robbers drive away. It might be that just *one* of all the witnesses noticed a crucial detail—like the license plate of the getaway car or the face of a robber when he took off his mask. Right after the crime, a detective can't always interview every single witness—he has to concentrate on the ones who saw everything or who might lead him to an immediate arrest. That's why he needs to get the name, address, and phone number of every witness, especially the ones he can't interview on the scene.

I've Got Your Number!

Stuff You'll Need
- **Watch or timer**
- **A piece of paper**
- **Notebook**
- **Pencil**

Pop quiz time, **detective rookies**! Can you remember what *Case File #3* is named and what it was all about? Try not to flip back the pages! If you can't remember it, never fear! We've got some great memory tricks to help you sharpen your skills!

A detective's memory is often crucial to solving cases. She has to keep all the facts of the case and all the things she has seen during the investigation in mind. When a detective interviews **witnesses**, she must remember what they say *and* what other witnesses she has talked to have told her. She may need to talk to four different witnesses, and see if their stories match! Not only does the detective have to *see* more than everyone else does at the scene of the crime, she also has to *remember* more clearly, too. Some people are born with great memories—others aren't—but anyone can learn to remember things better. There are a few tricks that detectives know…and *you* can use them, too!

There are two types of memory: long-term memory and short-term memory. Short-term memory holds details such as what you had for breakfast this morning or what you wore to school yesterday. Long-term memory is much less detailed, but lasts a long time. You probably don't remember what you had for breakfast a year ago, but you remember what grade you were in back then and what you studied in school (you *do* remember that…don't you?).

What You Do

Part I. Put It to the Test

One thing a witness might have to remember is the license plate number of a car. If a vehicle is speeding away from a **crime scene**, he might only have a few seconds to look at it. But those few seconds could be his only chance to find out—and remember—what was written on that plate. Test yourself to see if your memory is ready to record high-speed getaways, or if it needs to charge its batteries a bit.

1. To the right is a license plate. Look closely at it for 10 seconds. In your mind, repeat the numbers and letters, a few at a time.

2. Cover the plate with a piece of paper so you can't look at it, then try to recall the number. Write down the letters and numbers of the plate in your notebook.

CALIFORNIA

QLR 734

The Golden State

3. Check your answer. Did you get it right?

Part II. Chunk and Associate

One trick you can use to help you remember numbers is to group, or chunk, them together. It's easier to remember several groups of numbers than it is to remember a long list of individual ones. For example, think about the number 12253012. You could repeat that number to yourself several times, or you could divide it into smaller chunks like: 12 25 30 12. When the number is separated into parts, you no longer have to remember eight individual numbers; four groups of two is much easier, don't you think?

This technique works even better if you can separate a long number into chunks that are already familiar to you. That way, you can *associate* the numbers with something you know. In the numbers 12 25 30 12, the first two form 12/25, the date of Christmas. Hey, that's a number combo you can easily remember! What about 30 12? Or 301 2? Do those numbers mean anything to you? Can you connect them to your life? (For example, 30 might be your street number, and 12 might be your age.)

You can do the same thing with letters. If you come up with words that begin with each letter, you're much more likely to remember them. You can make up your own; for instance, if you saw a license plate DEOP45, you could create the phrase "Don't Eat Old Pie 45" and you'd probably be able to remember it for a while.

Take a look at the second license plate above, which is a little tougher to memorize than the first one. Use chunking and associating to help you remember it.

1. Divide the individual numbers and letters on this license plate into chunks. Write them in your notebook. (For example, J7X 11 09.)

2. Repeat the chunks to yourself three times.

3. Now, see if you can associate each chunk of digits with something else. In June, will your sister be 7 years old and will the next X-Men movie be coming out (for J7X)? Is 11/09 your dad's birthday? See if you can think of something in your life that relates to each of the number chunks.

4. Flip the page in your notebook, cover the plate with a piece of paper, then write down the numbers again as you remember them.

5. Check your answer. Were you able to remember the chunks? If not, repeat the numbers again, but this time say them out loud. By actually saying the numbers aloud, you're teaching them to your brain in two new ways: by forming them into words and by hearing them. This should make remembering easier.

Part III. Peg It!

If you attach *images* (mind pictures) to numbers or names, you can keep them in your memory for a long time. This can be as simple as using words and phrases that rhyme with the numbers you have to remember, or as complicated as associating a certain memory with certain numbers. You can use this technique to remember long numbers. A few examples should help make *pegging* clear:

1. Whether you know it or not, you've got an ID number that you've had since birth—a Social Security number. Have you got it memorized? What if your Social Security number is 118-22-3892. How do you remember it? You can rhyme 11 with the name *Kevin*. The number 8 sounds like the word *ate*. Then 2-2 rhymes with *blue glue*. And 3 rhymes with *she*, 8 with *ate*, and 92 sounds like *shiny glue*. So, what have you got? *Kevin ate blue glue. She ate shiny glue.* (Okay, Kevin isn't a *she*, but you get the idea.)

2. Cover up the number with a piece of paper. By saying the rhyme out loud, can you remember the number?

3. Ask a senior detective what *your* Social Security number is. Then come up with a peg to help you commit it to memory.

More From Detective Squad

Each state in the country issues its own license plate, and each state's plate is different (some states even have more than one style of license plates). It's important for detectives to be able to spot which state a license plate comes from, since the same number can be used by different states. Usually, the state is written above or below the number and there's some kind of picture on the plate. Different states also use their state colors on their plates. The next time you're traveling on the road, try playing this game, either by yourself or with others in the car. Keep a list of all the state plates you recognize. Can you spot all 50 states? That may take a *long* car ride! If you're playing this game with other passengers, can you find more state license plates than the other

Put your memory skills to use! Study these license plates for one minute, then turn the page and see if you can figure out which ones have changed. Ready? Go!

people in the car? The person who spots the plate first gets credit for that state. Eventually you'll be able to spot every plate in the country!

For more practice sharpening your memory, head to the Detective Academy website at www.scholastic.com/detective.

What's the Real Deal?

Fooled you! You already know the real deal—we started off with it this time! But we bet you were wondering why we used license plates for you to memorize?

Detectives do a lot of *surveillance*, which means they follow and watch people who are **suspects**, or they watch places where crimes have frequently occurred. What are you going to do when the person you're watching jumps in a strange car and speeds off? You're going to memorize the license plate, that's what!

JUST THE FACTS

No More Numbers!

It's not an accident that phone numbers are only seven digits long (like 555-3897). Studies have shown that most people can easily remember numbers that have seven digits, but not more. Besides your home phone number, you've probably memorized quite a few others. How many digits or combos of numbers and letters are in a license plate? No more than seven, right? Case proven!

NEW MEXICO
D7M1A0
Grand Canyon State

B1ANC4
COLORADO

FLORIDA
JAR4MY
SUNSHINE STATE

illinois   Land of Lincoln
D0T4CT4

KANSAS
T7H5M3

MISSOURI
G3ZR10
SHOW-ME STATE

NEW YORK
O74 R1E

TEXAS
W33✦1N0

OCEAN STATE
MAL398
RHODE ISLAND

What differences did you notice in these license plates compared to the ones on page 29?

Tell It Like It Is

You've got a bunch of **witnesses** to a crime and they all saw what happened. Case closed, right? Not so fast, **rookie**. People don't always see things the same way. For example, you'd think that the height and weight of a criminal a witness saw at the scene of a crime would be easy to get right. But it isn't! Often, witnesses give different descriptions of the same **suspect**. See for yourself how this can happen.

Stuff You'll Need
- Pencil
- At least two friends
- Disguise materials (like different shoes, colored T-shirts, or eyeliner to make fake moles)

What You Do

Part I. Weight a Minute!

A good way to estimate someone's height and weight is to mentally compare them to your own. Start by entering your height and weight in the box here.

My Height	
My Weight	

1. Now, get together with a couple of your friends or fellow rookie **detectives**. Write each friend's name in the column on the grid below, then guess each person's height and weight. Add those numbers to the chart. If your best friend is a little taller than you are, take your height and add a few inches to it. Do the same thing with your weight. If your friend is thinner than you, deduct pounds from your weight.

2. Now ask your friends to tell you their actual height and weight. Then add it to the chart. Were your estimates close?

3. Keep at it, but vary the game a little. Try guessing the height and weight of your five-year-old cousin, your teacher, or even a professional basketball player. It's not so easy when the person is a very different size than you are!

Part II. Surprise!

One of the things that distorts witnesses' perceptions of what happened in a crime is surprise or shock. Witnesses to a violent or sudden crime may have very different descriptions of the **perpetrator**.

1. Tell two or more of your friends that you're going to surprise them within the next few days when you're all together, but don't tell them how or exactly when.

Friend's Name	Estimated Height	Actual Height	Estimated Weight	Actual Weight

31

2. When you know you'll all be together somewhere (like hanging out at your house), dress up in a way that has some odd feature (maybe wear two different shoes or a fake mole on your face) and surprise them. Jump on the scene. Give a shout. (Don't say, "boo!" Try something original.) Then snatch something from the room where they are, like the TV remote control. Quickly leave the scene, change back to your original attire, and rejoin your friends.

3. Now that you've changed back to your normal clothing, question each friend separately. Ask them to describe what they saw. Are there differences in your friends' stories? How do they describe how you looked and what you did? Do they agree on what you said? Bring your friends back together and share the differences in their stories with them.

4. Was that easy or hard? Try surprising your friends again (wait until they aren't expecting it—don't do it right after your first attempt), but this time when you surprise them, wear your normal clothes. When you leave the room *after* you surprise them, change your clothes, but make the changes in your dress more subtle (for example, this time change from a black T-shirt to a gray one). Do your friends notice the subtle difference in your clothing?

What's the Real Deal?

Don't be discouraged if your estimates were off by a lot when you guessed your friends' heights and weights in *Part I*. This is a skill that police officers start learning the moment they join the force. They may be pretty good at it by the time they make detective, but it really takes years to perfect. A good start is always to know your *own* height and weight. That way, you can compare someone else's size to your own, and come up with a reasonably accurate estimate.

When detectives are investigating a crime with multiple witnesses (like you did in *Part II*), one of the first things they do is separate those witnesses as soon as possible. They do this so that the witnesses can't talk to each other about what they saw and adjust their stories so that they match. It's just a natural thing people do—subconsciously filling in the blanks of what they saw with what the other person saw. Once the detective has the statements from different witnesses, he'll try to put the info together into a coherent description of the events of the crime and the perpetrators.

DET. HIGH-TECH!

Mug Shot Software

One of the tools detectives have at their disposal is a computer that has photographs of frequent offenders sorted by description. Once they have a general description of a criminal—say they know that he's around 6' 2", tall, male, white, and about

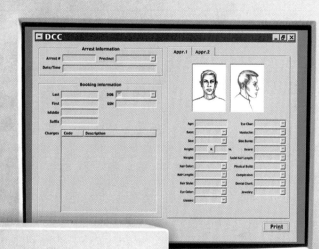

200 pounds—they can program the computer to show the witness every person in the local area who matches that description and has committed a crime like the one the witness saw. Many cases have been solved this way.

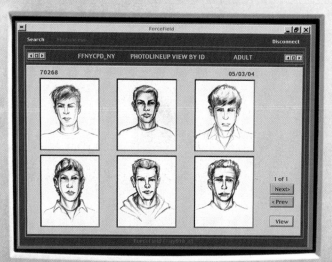

How would you describe these suspects? How are they alike? Different?

Det. is an abbreviation for detective!

Body Talk))))

How reliable is that **witness** you're talking to? Check out his body language! The same can be said for a **suspect**. Does she seem nervous when she talks to you? Like she's on edge? Or perhaps she seems overly sincere?

Most people don't realize—or can't control—what their body does when they're talking. Ever see someone and just know at a glance that they were really tired? How did you know? Probably because their eyes were drooping or they were rubbing their eyes, or they were yawning—dead giveaways that they were in need of some sleep!

Good **detectives** become aware of even the most subtle movements a person (be it a witness or a suspect) makes. These little clues are usually subconscious—meaning the person doesn't even realize he's doing them. So while the suspect might be saying "yes" to a question you ask him, he might look away from you when he answers, suggesting his answer is really "no" instead. Warm up your body language skills in this activity.

What You Do

Part I. Charades!

1. Practice using body language to communicate with your friends. Start with something obvious: Pretend you have a stomach ache! Are you holding your stomach in pain? Is your face scrunched up in a grimace? Don't tell the other players what you're acting out, and see if they can tell what's wrong with you.

2. Now move on to something more subtle. Place a pebble in your shoe—don't exaggerate the effect, just behave as you would if you weren't playing a game. Do your friends notice your limp?

3. Have your friends come up with body language charades of their own for you to figure out.

Walking as if you had a limp.

Part II. Emotion Speaks

Now that you're getting good at noticing physical things that are shown through body language, it's time to learn about the more *subtle* ways in which the body can talk to you about your suspects—through their *emotions*.

Looking angry.

1. Make a list of emotions in your notebook that a suspect might be feeling, such as *anger*, *fear*, *anxiety*, *rage*, or *pride*. If you were talking to a suspect who was acting out one of these emotions, would you be suspicious?

Looking fearful.

2. Have a friend choose one of these emotions and, without naming it, act it out. What would someone who's *anxious* look like? They could be biting their nails and tensing up their muscles. Have the other players ask him questions to see if they can guess what emotion he is representing. For example, say, "Tell me everything you did yesterday." The player responds while keeping his emotion in mind. If the player is acting out being *angry*, for example, she might snap, "I can't *possibly* remember everything I did yesterday!"

What's the Real Deal?

Think about the different emotions that were just acted out. If you were interviewing a suspect and you got the feeling she was showing signs of, say, fear—what might that tell you? Do you think someone who's fearful of being questioned by a detective might be hiding something? Maybe...but she also might be afraid of the police because she just got a speeding ticket the day before. Whenever detectives interview someone—whether they're a suspect or a witness—they ask a lot of questions that might seem unrelated to the case. They aren't being nosy (well, maybe they *are*, but that's their job, after all!); they're trying to sense what the suspect might be feeling. In fact, there are classes run by agencies like the Federal Bureau of Investigation (FBI) and large police departments across the country about reading people's emotions during questioning. The methods involve not just knowing what the person is feeling, but also knowing how to *get them* to feel certain emotions that can make them be more truthful. For example, if you wanted to get someone angry, you might ask them personal questions or insult them—just enough so that they get worked up! When you watch a detective who really knows this technique and has conducted thousands of interviews, it's almost as if he has ESP (the power to read someone's mind)!

CRIME in Fiction

SHERLOCK HOLMES AND THE POWER OF DEDUCTION

In 1887 in England, a talented writer named Sir Arthur Conan Doyle created perhaps the most famous of all fictional detectives: Sherlock Holmes.

Here's a description of Holmes in his own words from *A Study in Scarlet*, written in 1887:

"'I have a turn both for observation and for deduction.... I'm a consulting detective.... Here in London we have lots of government detectives and lots of private ones. When these fellows are at fault, they come to me, and I manage to put them on the right scent. They lay all the evidence before me, and I am generally able, by the help of my knowledge of the history of crime, to set them straight. There is a strong family resemblance about misdeeds, and if you have all the details of a thousand [crimes] at your finger ends, it is odd if you can't unravel the thousand and first.'"

Ok, so Sherlock Holmes thinks he's a great detective, but is he really? Check out this scene. Watson—Holmes's sidekick and the "I" in the narrative below—is always surprised by how easily Holmes can figure things out...even when Watson tries to set him up to fail!

"'I have heard you say it is difficult for a man to have any object in daily use without leaving the impress of his individuality upon it in such a way that a trained observer might read it. Now, I have here a watch which has recently come into my possession. Would you have the kindness to let me have an opinion upon the character or habits of the late owner?'

I handed [Holmes] over the watch with some slight feeling of amusement in my heart, for the test was, as I thought, an impossible one.... He balanced the watch in his hand, gazed

hard at the dial, opened the back, and examined the works, first with his naked eyes and then with a powerful convex lens. I could hardly keep from smiling at his crestfallen face when he finally snapped the case and handed it back.

'There are hardly any data,' he remarked. 'The watch has been recently cleaned, which robs me of my most suggestive facts.'

'You are right,' I answered. 'It was cleaned before being sent to me.'

In my heart I accused my companion of putting forward a most lame...excuse to cover a failure. What data could be expected from an uncleaned watch?

'Though unsatisfactory, my research has not been entirely barren,' [Holmes] observed.... 'Subject to your correction, I should judge that the watch belonged to your elder brother, who inherited it from your father.'

'That you gather, no doubt, from the H.W. upon the back?'

'Quite so. The W. suggests your own name. The date of the watch is nearly fifty years back and the initials are as old as the watch: so it was made for the last generation. Jewellery usually descends to the eldest son, and he is most likely to have the same name as the father. Your father has, if I remember right, been dead many years. It has, therefore, been in the hands of your eldest brother.

'Right so far,' said I. 'Anything else?'

'He was a man of untidy habits—very untidy and careless. He was left with good prospects, but he threw away his chances....'

I sprang from my chair and limped impatiently about the room with considerable bitterness in my heart."

So much for that! Even when set up Holmes can figure out everything!

Motive, Motive, Motive

In *Case File #8: Body Talk*, you practiced figuring out what a **suspect** might be *feeling* after a crime. What a suspect feels is a clue to why he might commit a crime—his **motive**. A motive can be simple and easy to understand or it can be strange and make sense only to the criminal. But understanding the motive behind a crime, or at least figuring out what it is, can often help solve a case and convict a criminal. One thing's for sure: If a person committed a crime, he had a motive. And the sooner you figure out what it is, the better!

What You Do

Part I. The Case of the Missing Painting

1. You're a **detective** called to the local art museum where a valuable painting has been stolen. The painting was small and could possibly have been carried off in someone's coat. You've rounded up four suspects who had the opportunity to steal the painting. The *manager* of the museum is a suspect—he opened the museum in the morning and said he found the painting gone. The *security guard* is a suspect—he was in the museum all night. A *pickpocket* who usually works the area is considered a suspect because he was recently seen at the museum. And an *art buff* who was seen at closing time near where the painting hung is your last suspect.

You interview the manager and he tells you that he hated the painter's work. If it were up to him, he wouldn't have displayed the painting at all, but a wealthy patron of the museum donated it and the manager felt obligated to exhibit it. He also tells you that he thinks it was probably the security guard who did it since he was about to be fired for sleeping on the job.

You interview the security guard and he tells you that he's in debt and can't afford to lose his job. He also tells you that he thinks it was probably the pickpocket who stole the painting because he is, after all, a thief.

The pickpocket tells you that, yes, he was in the museum looking for pockets to pick, but he didn't steal anything. He also tells you that he saw the art buff hanging around the painting when he was in the museum, so it was probably him.

37

The art buff, who is moved to tears by the theft, tells you that he visits the museum every day and loves the painter's work. He's devastated at the theft of the painting, but says it probably wasn't taken by the manager because he has lousy taste in art.

2. Jot down each suspect's name in your notebook, along with a checklist of each person's motive. The list has been started for you.

[Notebook:]

Suspect	Motive
1-Manager	hates the painting
2-Security Guard	

Part II. Find the Culprit

Looking at the list of suspects and motives you just made, is there one suspect who stands out? Motive alone won't solve a case for you, but it *can* point you in the right direction. There *is* one suspect who you should probably concentrate on in your investigation. Can you figure out who he is? Check out *Case Closed* to see if you're right.

More From Detective Squad

Anytime you hear about a crime, ask yourself, "Why would someone do that?" Sometimes you'll be halfway toward figuring out who did it when you answer that question!

What's the Real Deal?

Ideally, detectives would interview the "**witnesses**" (that is, *potential* **perpertrators**) back at the detective squad as soon as possible after the crime was discovered. Each person would be asked to write down what they were doing before and after the crime occurred and what their feelings about the crime were. That way, someone might have revealed their motive in writing before they even knew that they were actually a suspect! Detectives can check a person's answers to questions asked later against his initial statement. If detectives *do* discover inconsistencies, it's further **evidence**, and it will allow them to concentrate more on that suspect. But just like a motive, a suspect's inconsistencies is just a piece of the puzzle and doesn't yet mean the case is solved!

CASE IN POINT
A Noble Motive?

In April 2003, three paintings by Picasso, Van Gogh, and Gauguin, valued at over $1.5 million, were stolen from the Whitworth Art Gallery in Manchester, England. As the police conducted their investigation into who might have stolen the paintings, they received an anonymous tip by telephone. A female caller told them that the paintings had been taken, not as a crime, but to illustrate the inadequate security at the art museum. The caller then told the police where the paintings could be found. The police recovered the stolen art, but the case still hasn't been resolved, since no arrests have been made. Do you think employees of the museum might be the culprits? Is it possible that the stated motive was a lie and the thieves got nervous and abandoned the loot? Or do you think their motive—teaching the museum about security—was a "noble" one?

The Whitworth Art Gallery in England.

Detective, Where Are You?

Stuff You'll Need
- Pencil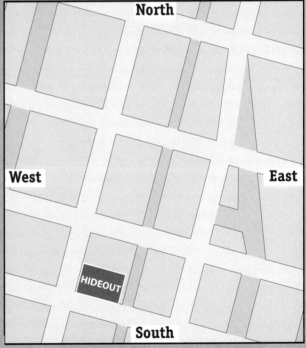
- Plastic wrap, a small piece
- Red permanent marker
- Ruler
- Flashlight
- Tape
- Notebook

One of the things that **detectives** and police officers learn very early in their careers is a simple rule: *Always know where you are.* Why is that so important? Detectives need to be able to describe their locations easily, so they can tell other detectives where they are in case they need help. Also, if they're checking out a **suspect**, they might need to follow him to an area they're not familiar with. So how do they always know where they are? One way is by getting in the habit of looking up at the street signs and making mental notes of the intersection where they are. The other way is by carrying a map with them at all times. One of the things you'll find in every detective squad in the world is a detailed map of the area. Get ready to practice your map skills with this case!

What You Do

Part I. Find Your Way

1. Look at the map here. You'll notice the directions north, south, east, and west. You'll need these basic directions to know how to read a map and figure out where you are. On this map, streets either run north-south or east-west.

2. Of the two large streets that run up and down (or north and south) on the map, the one to the left (or west) is Broadway. The one to the right (or east) is Lafayette Street. Label them. Broadway and Lafayette Street run *parallel* to each other (meaning they run next to each other and never cross).

3. Of the streets that run across (or east and west) on the map, the east-west street farthest to the north is Prince Street. One block south of Prince is Spring Street. One block south of Spring is Broome Street, and one block south

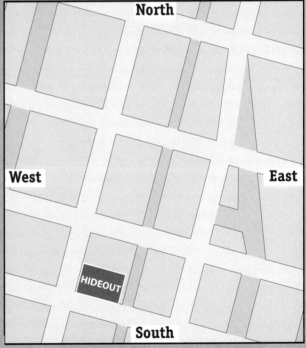

of Broome is Grand Street. Label these streets on the map. These streets run parallel to each other and *perpendicular* (meaning they cross each other at right angles) to Broadway and Lafayette Street.

4. Now imagine you've found a suspect's hideout and have marked it on your map. You need to call the police station to get some help with the arrest. Look at the map. At the intersection of which two streets will you tell them you are located? Check out *Case Closed*.

Part II. Save Your Night Vision

Imagine you're looking at a map at night and trying to find someone in the dark. If you use your flashlight to look at the map, your eyes will adjust to the bright light and you won't be able to see well when you look around the dark streets. There's a trick that detectives use for exactly this situation.

1. Take a piece of plastic wrap and a red permanent marker. Color a red circle about an inch and a half in diameter on the plastic wrap.

2. Put the plastic wrap over the top of the flashlight so the red circle covers the lens. Use tape to secure the plastic wrap to the head of the flashlight.

3. Bring your new red light and this book into a dark room and wait until your eyes adjust to the dark.

4. See how easy it is to read the book with the red light and still see in the dark room? That's because red light doesn't spoil your night vision...it actually helps it!

Part III.
Put Your New Light to Work

1. Now go out in your neighborhood in the evening (have a senior detective go with you). Bring your red light and your notebook and pencil. (If you prefer to do this in the daytime, you won't need your red light.)

2. Use your red light and draw a simple map of your neighborhood. Do you know your neighborhood as well as you think you do?

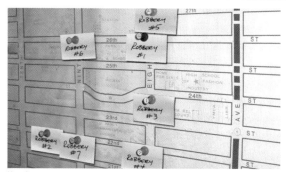

Here's a map from a police precinct that shows where robberies have recently been committed in the area. This is an example of where your map-reading skills come in handy!

More From Detective Squad

When detectives are looking for suspects, sometimes they need to be quiet so the suspects won't know that they're there. But they still need to communicate with each other. Use your flashlight to signal to fellow rookie detectives. You can use your red light at night since it won't be as noticeable to a suspect. One flash (turning your flashlight on and off quickly) might mean "help." Two flashes might mean "everything is okay." Three might mean "keep your head down." Make up your own signals to communicate with your friends.

Want more map practice? Log on to the Detective Academy website at www.scholastic.com/detective.

What's the Real Deal?

Not only do detectives pay attention to where they are at all times, they also have a quick way to call for help in a real emergency to let other detectives know where they are. If a detective uses his police radio and simply gives an intersection or an address with no other explanation (like "Broadway and Spring!"), the other detectives know that what he means is "I'm at Broadway and Spring and I need help right away."

One of the tools that has been built into police cars is a red light, which works like the one you made in *Part II*. When you open the door of the police car, a light comes on inside, just like in regular cars. But a police car's interior lights can be switched to red so that the detectives and police officers can get their gear or look at maps in the dark without hurting their night vision. After practicing with the red light in *Parts II* and *III*, you know just how that works!

HOLLYWOOD IT'S NOT!

Think you've seen enough TV shows and movies to know what detective work is all about? Think again! TV shows like *CSI, NYPD Blue, Law & Order*, and even old classics like *Dragnet* portray detectives doing glamorous and exciting work. But there are big differences between what you see on the screen and what goes on in real life. As you learn more about being a detective, you, too, will begin to see where Hollywood has exaggerated what really goes on.

Hollywood Fantasy #1: *Violence.* While detective work can be dangerous, there's nowhere near as much violence involved in detective work as Hollywood pretends there is. Still, detectives can find themselves in dangerous situations. To stay safe, they spend a lot of time planning how to conduct investigations and arrest people as safely as possible. Most detectives in the United States carry guns, but very few of them have to fire them in the line of duty. In fact, the *last* thing a detective really wants is to have to use his gun. Detectives prefer to use their heads!

Hollywood Fantasy #2: *Paperwork.* It probably wouldn't be very interesting to watch a show about someone who just sat around and filled out a lot of paperwork, but that's actually what detectives spend a lot of time doing! Detectives need to write down everything that happens in an investigation…*everything*. All the evidence needs to be cataloged and described. All the interviews need to be written out, word by word, into reports. All of the places that a detective goes and things that he sees need to be written down. Why all the notes? When a suspect is arrested and brought to trial, the detective has to be able to show the court *exactly* what lead him to believe that the suspect was, in fact, the perpetrator of the crime. His reports are also used by his fellow detectives so that they can help with the investigation. In addition, his lieutenant needs to be able to check his work to make sure he's doing what he's supposed to be doing (and not sitting in McDonald's instead!).

Take away all the violence and add all the paperwork and you've got a TV show that gets two thumbs down! But when you're a real detective working to solve a difficult case, nothing could be more exciting!

41

Making Dark Into Light

When you're looking for **suspects**, it won't always be in broad daylight. In fact, crimes are often committed under the cover of darkness both because it's tougher for the **perpetrators** to be seen and because most people usually don't work in their offices or stores at night—making it easier for crimes to take place. But **detectives** like the nighttime as much as criminals do! At night, it's easier to keep an eye on a suspect because *you* can stay out of sight, too. It can also be easier to spot suspects, since there are usually less people out at night.

Our eyes don't work the same in the dark as they do during the day. In order to become adept at searching for suspects at night, a detective has to learn how to use his night vision better than the average person—so he can spot the bad guys before the bad guys spot him!

What You Do

Part I. Can You See in the Dark?

You can, but you have to let your eyes *adjust* first. Try this game.

1. Invite a friend over to your house and have him hide in a dark room while you wait in a *well-lit* hallway.

2. Quickly go into the dark room and see how long it takes you to find your friend. Imagine being a detective trying to find a suspect when the suspect's eyes are adjusted to the dark and yours aren't. That's a dangerous situation!

Part II. Even the Playing Field

1. Now have your friend hide in a dark room again while you wait in a *dark* hallway.

2. Make sure your eyes have adjusted to the dark before you go into the room to look for him.

3. How long does it take to find your friend this time?

Part III. Flash!

1. Like you did in *Part II*, hang out in a dark hallway while your friend is in a dark room hiding.

2. Wait until your eyes have adjusted to the dark.

3. This time, when you go into the room, use your red light from *Case File #10: Detective, Where Are You?* to see if you can find him even more quickly than before. Is it easier for you to find your friend than it was in *Part II*?

What's the Real Deal?

Inside your eye there's a lens just like in a camera. When you're in the sunlight or a room where there's lots of light, this opening (called your *pupil*) gets very small so that only a little light goes in your eye and you don't blind yourself. When you're out at night or in a dark room, your pupils get very large to let as much light in as they can to help you see. Ever go from a dark building out into a sunny day? You squint to protect your eyes while your pupils contract to get used to the change in light. The expanding and contracting of your pupils happen quickly and automatically, but it still takes a few minutes before your eyes become fully adjusted.

When you went from the well-lit hallway into the dark room in *Part I*, your eyes didn't get a chance to adjust and your night vision was poor. In *Part II*, your eyes were already adjusted to the dark and you probably found your friend much more quickly than in *Part I*. That's why detectives always have to be mindful of their night vision. In *Part III*, by letting your eyes get used to the dark and then using your red light, it should have been even easier for you to find your friend than in *Part II*. Nobody wants to be all alone in the dark— not even detectives! Before searching a dark **crime scene**, detectives often call for backup from fellow detectives with bigger and brighter flashlights!

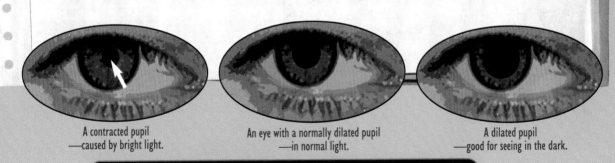

A contracted pupil —caused by bright light.

An eye with a normally dilated pupil —in normal light.

A dilated pupil —good for seeing in the dark.

Why do you think cats can see so well in the dark?
Do you think their pupils have something to do with it?

On the Job: At Work
With Detective Luke Miller

Detective Luke heading into the precinct where he works.

My favorite assignment as a **detective** for the New York City Police Department (NYPD) was at the 10th Precinct. The 10th covers an area known as Chelsea, in Manhattan, New York. The neighborhood is diverse, with expensive shops and fancy places to live, along with some other more crime-prone areas. What really made it a great place to work was the other detectives in the squad. We had detectives with over 20 years experience who knew the job inside and out, as well as police officers who were recently assigned to the squad in hopes of getting the promotion to detective. When I arrived for a typical day at the squad, I would greet my two partners, Mike Glynn and Rob "Tank" Tancredi. Mike and I were already detectives and Rob was up for promotion to detective any day. The 10th Precinct is a small one—only nine detectives total—so the three of us made up a whole team.

On the streets of New York, Detective Luke makes his way to meet a witness for an interview.

We'd start the day by sitting down with the detectives who'd been working the shift before us (sometimes it was 7 a.m., sometimes it was 4 p.m.). They'd tell us if any major cases had come in during their shift and if anything was left over for us to take care of. If there was nothing pressing, the three of us would come up with a plan for the shift. It might include time for calling **witnesses** to cases we were working on or plans to go out and pick up **evidence**, such as a

Making calls at his desk—Detective Lu on the phone with a witness, arranging him to come in.

surveillance video from a store that had been burglarized. Once we'd caught up on casework, we'd go look for **suspects** that were wanted for arrest or who we wanted to interview. The plan for the day would also include what we were having for lunch or dinner. Our supervisor was a **sergeant** named Greg Kelly. He was a big guy and had lots of experience in the police department, so he was good to have with us in case of trouble. Ideally, one of us would crack a case and arrest a suspect, and our evening plans would change. The meal would have to wait while we did all the paperwork that detectives have to do when they arrest people. We'd have to search, interview, and fingerprint the prisoner; and then we'd arrange a ride for the prisoner down to court. If no arrest was made, we'd brief the next shift and head home.

At a crime scene, Detective Luke takes a first look around.

You've been working on your observation skills throughout this book, but how observant are you really? Who is Luke Miller? Where have you seen his name before? Check out *Case Closed.*

Case of the Computer Burglar

Well, **rookie**, by this time you should have a pretty good feel for some of the basics of **detective** work. You now know a bit about how to search a **crime scene** for clues and what to do when you find fingerprints or **trace evidence**. You know you can continue an investigation by interviewing **witnesses** and **suspects**, by checking their statements for important facts, and by looking for signals that they might be lying. You know how to look for **motives** for crimes. And you know tricks to help your memory and your night vision.

But there's much more ahead, as you'll see in future Detective Academy books. Still, you'll want to keep the *Basic Training Manual* handy as you move on to the more advanced topics that are coming up (in case you need to refer back to the basic techniques of detective work). But while you get ready for next month's book and gadgets, here's one more case for you to solve (and it's based on a real crime).

On May 5, 2000, the Aguilar Computer Technology Company was burglarized. In the middle of the night, a man broke in and loaded up a mail cart with approximately $20,000 worth of new computers.

Look closely at the picture of the burglar as he's in the elevator ready to depart with his stolen computers. What clues would you search for at this crime scene? What do the clues tell you about the crime and the person who's committing it? What might his motive be? Look carefully at what the man has with him and what's in the elevator. Now flip back through this book and try to use some of the techniques you've learned to answer all these questions. As always, your best asset is your mind and your power of observation...so look at the picture closely. What else could you do to bring this crime scene to life? Would fingerprints help? Where would you start looking for prints? Use your magnifying glass to take an extra-close look.

Write down who you think this **perpetrator** is, and how he managed to commit the crime. Then, turn to *Case Closed* to see how you matched up to the real detectives!

 Want more cases like this to solve? Head to the Detective Academy website at www.scholastic.com/detective!

WHO'S WHO?

Luke Miller is a **detective** with the New York Police Department (NYPD). In his 13 years on the job, he's worked on patrol, undercover in the narcotics division, as a **precinct** detective, and in the intelligence division. In addition to police work, he's a frequent contributor to Slate—an online magazine—where he has a column called "Flatfoot."

H. Keith Melton is a well-known expert on detective and spy history, tradecraft, and forensics. He's the author of four books, including *The Ultimate Spy*, which is currently used as an introductory manual for new employees of the CIA. He is an advisor to U.S. intelligence agencies and a professor at the Counter-intelligence Centre in Alexandria, Virginia, where he lectures on espionage and counterterrorism. He also has a collection of more than 7,000 detective and spy devices, books, and documents.

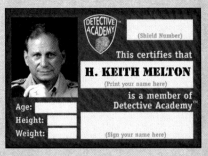

Paul Mauro is a **sergeant** with the New York City Police Department.

UP AND COMING

Want to know what you can expect in future months as you continue on your way to becoming a professional detective? Here's a sneak peek:

Crime Scene Investigation

Forensics: Trace Evidence and DNA

Interviewing Witnesses and Interrogating Suspects

Collecting and Handling Evidence

Print Analysis

And so much more!

CASE CLOSED

Women "On The Job" *(page 10)*

Women make great detectives for lots of reasons. But they can be better than men sometimes because when they're working undercover, suspects don't think they're detectives!

What Happened Here...and Who Did It?
(page 13)

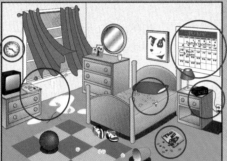

Did you notice the *squirrelly* evidence? So what happened in this room? A window was left open while a family went on vacation for a week (note the calendar on the wall). A small animal—possibly a squirrel—made itself at home in the bedroom, running back and forth across the bed, chewing on the bedspread and pillow, and snacking on trail mix (that's why the pack is torn open in the middle). It even left part of his lunch (an acorn) on the windowsill. The wind and a rainstorm blew water, leaves, and twigs into the room, a clear sign that no one was home to close the window. During the storm, the electricity must have gone out, since the plugged-in clock on the night table and the battery-operated clock on the wall (notice: no cord!) don't show the same time. How did you do? Don't worry if you didn't pick all that up, rookie. We're just getting started!

Case File #1: Trained Eyes *(page 15)*

What five things changed?

1. The basketball was moved to the floor.
2. The potato chips were moved to the desk and eaten.
3. The drawer was closed.
4. Some of the CDs were moved to the floor.
5. The book was opened on the desk.

Case File #3: As Small As The Eye Can See
(page 20)

Want to know the secret message? Well, we're not going to tell you yet! You've got to wait until the end of the book! Turn to page 48.

Case File #4: Magnification Investigation
(page 22)

Part I. Prints **A** and **F** are the good prints.

Case File #5: You Saw What?
(pages 24–26)

Just the Facts:

Abbreviations:

- perps—perpetrators
- B/M—black male
- yrs—years
- lbs—pounds
- BB—baseball
- W/M—white male
- Brn—brown
- H/M—Hispanic male

Part III. Here's what we know about the case so far, as written by a detective:

Case Report	Detective's Name and Shield Number:
Today's Date:	Crime: Bank Robbery
Location (this is the *Where*): First National Savings Bank	
Time of Occurrence (this is the *When*): Approximately 10:00 am	
Method of Crime (this is the *What* and *How*—describe what you believe happened): Perpetrators entered the location. One displayed a handgun. Second perp produced a sack and made a statement similar to, "Put all the money in the bag!" Perps then left location, entered a green Volkswagen Bug, and fled scene in vehicle. No injuries reported.	
Perpetrators/Suspects (this is the *Who*): Perp #1: Male, approximately 5 feet 2 inches tall. Perp #2: Male, heavily built. Faces not seen by witnesses. Both perps wore white shirts, black trousers, and brown work boots.	
Names of Witnesses (this is also the *Who*): #1—Ms. Brittany Jones, female, age 18. #2—Mr. Al Smith, male, age 51.	
Property Taken (this is the *What* and the *Why*. What was stolen? If nothing, then why was the crime committed? What was the motive?): Cash from bank removed by perps.	
Case Status (circle one):	(Open) Closed by Arrest

47

CASE CLOSED

(continued

Case File #9: Motive, Motive, Motive (pages 37–38)

Part I. Manager: His motive is that he hates the artist's work. It might be easy for him to remove the painting without having to take the blame since he is the museum manager.

Security Guard: He is in debt, which means he needs money, and he is about to lose his job.

Pickpocket: He is a known thief and he obviously likes to steal things.

Art Buff: He loves the artist's work and he might want the painting for himself.

Part II. The security guard has a triple motive; he needs the money to pay off debts, he is about to be fired, and he is about to lose the opportunity to take the painting because he's about to be fired. His motives are both stronger and more likely to motivate him to crime than the other suspects. That doesn't *prove* he's the perpetrator, but a good detective will concentrate on him, until or unless more compelling information or evidence is discovered.

Case File #10: Detective, Where Are You? (pages 39–40)

Part I. The suspect's hideout is on the corner of Broadway and Grand Street. Go find him!

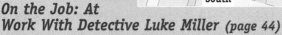

On the Job: At Work With Detective Luke Miller (page 44)

Luke Miller is one of the authors of this book! You can find his name on the title page and again in the *Who's Who?* section on page 46.

Case of the Computer Burglar (page 45)

A tough case to be sure (especially for a rookie!).

✓ The most important item in the picture is the video camera in the corner of the elevator. Did you notice it? Many buildings have security cameras, and a detective will get the surveillance video. The tape won't reveal the identity of the burglar, but with it you'll at least have his picture.

✓ The company keys in the man's hand and the mail cart are clues that the burglar might know his way around the Aguilar Computer Technology Company pretty well. It's likely that he's an employee or a former employee!

✓ As for fingerprints: The bottom elevator button has one on it.

This actual case was solved by detectives who showed the videotape of the burglary to company employees. The employees noticed that, even though the burglar's face was tough to see on the tape, the man looked like a former employee of the company (in fact, one who had recently been fired for stealing company property). Revenge on the company that fired him would be a pretty strong motive for someone already in the habit of stealing.

The burglar wore gloves when he came into the building. But in the picture, you see that one glove is off—he left a fingerprint on the elevator button. The identification by the other employees was enough evidence to lead detectives to the suspect, and the fingerprint match became the basis for his arrest. Faced with the evidence, the employee confessed and was sentenced to three years in prison.

Did you figure all that out? Don't worry if you didn't—you probably got at least some of it. Keep practicing your skills, rookie, and you'll be a great detective one day, too!

Secret Message:

You're on your way to becoming a great detective! "You're" is on page 20; "on" is on page 34; "your" is on page 41; "way" is on page 44; "to" is on page 27; "becoming" is on page 31; "a" is on page 37; "great" is on page 24; "detective!" is on page 10.